LANGUAGE
AND HOW TO
USE IT

BOOK 2

Andrew Schiller
Marion Monroe
Ralph Nichols
William Jenkins
Charlotte Huck

SCOTT, FORESMAN AND COMPANY

Contents

6 The Authors

SECTION ONE

9 Let's Talk

10 How Big Is Big?

11 A Story

12 Rhymes and Nonsense

14 Look and Tell

15 Tell What's Happening

16 Let's Listen

17 A Story

18 Feelings

19 Telling and Asking

20 Sentences

22 Word Order

23 Look and Think

24 What Did They Say?

26 Telling Stories

28 Poems

30 Words for What We Do and Did

31 A Story

32 Let's Listen

SECTION TWO

34 What Are They Like?

36 Why Rabbit Has a Short Tail

38 Riddle Me, Riddle Me, What Is That?

40 Word Order

42 Let's Listen

44 A Story

45 Writing a Story

46 Opposites

48 Giving Directions

49 Let's Listen

50 Which Word?

52 Look and Think

53 Let's Listen

54 Let's Think About Words

56 A Poem

57 Play the Sentence Game

58 Words That Name Sounds

60 Poems

62 A Poem

SECTION THREE

64   **Letter Writing**

67   **A Poem**

68   **Making Sentences**

70   **Be a Word Collector**

72   **A Poem**

74   **If I Were . . .**

75   **Let's Listen**

76   **A Poem**

78   **Using Different Words**

79   **Let's Listen**

80   **Asking or Telling**

81   **A Poem**

82   **A Puppet Show**

83   **Let's Listen**

84   **Finishing Sentences**

86   **Where Is It?**

88   **The Golden Goose**

91   **Some Words Help Tell Where or When**

92   **Writing Stories**

94   **Answer the Questions**

96   **Look and Think**

SECTION FOUR

98 A Modern Ballad

100 How Do You Know It's Spring?

102 Punctuation

104 A Weary Word

106 A Poem

108 A Story

109 Words Describe

110 Writing Invitations

112 Let's Listen

113 Look and Write

114 Poems

116 Stories to Finish

118 Making Sentences

119 Let's Listen

120 Punctuation

122 An Old Car Picnic

124 Working with Words

125 Let's Listen

126 The Sentence Game

127 Look and Think

Andrew Schiller
University of Illinois at Chicago Circle
College of Liberal Arts and Sciences
Department of English
Professor and Chairman of Linguistics

Marion Monroe
Formerly University of Southern California
Director of Reading Clinic

The
Authors

Ralph Nichols
University of Minnesota
Department of Rhetoric
Department Head

William A. Jenkins
Portland State University
School of Education
Professor of Education and Dean

Charlotte S. Huck
The Ohio State University
College of Education
Professor of Education

6

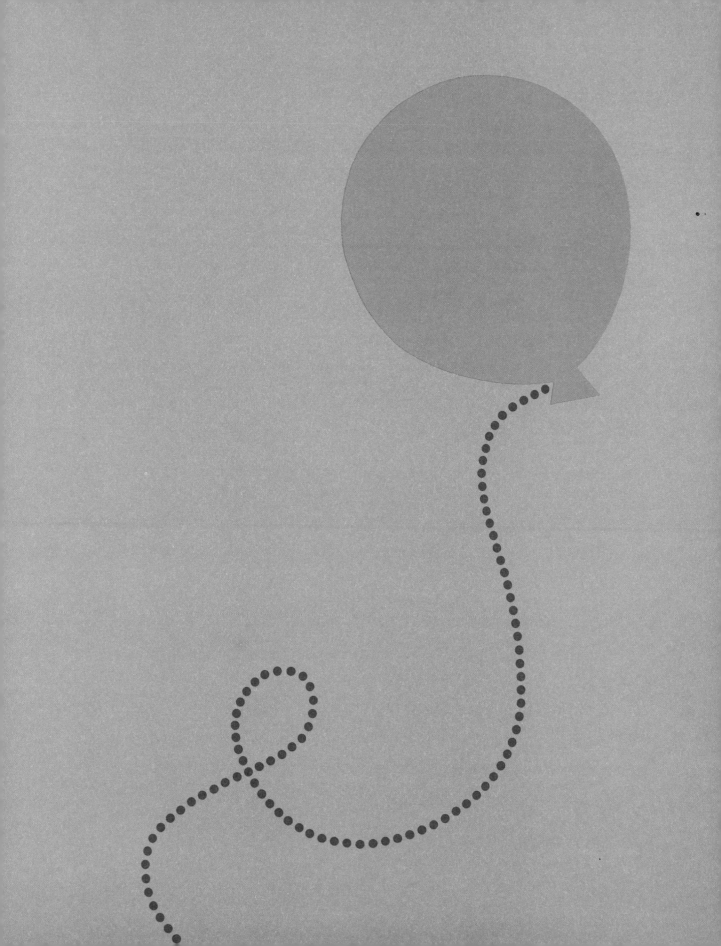

Let's Talk

Have you seen anything interesting
or unusual or funny recently? Tell about
it. It need not be as big as an elephant.
It can be something as little as a poodle
or a pigeon or two ants having a tug-
of-war with a crumb.

9

How Big Is Big?

Which animal is biggest?
Which animal is smallest?
How can elephants be both big and little?
When is the smallest animal big?
When do you feel big?
When do you feel little?

A Story

Talk

Tell the story.
Play the story.

Rhymes
and
Nonsense

It's a Little Awkward
by Marci Ridlon

A mole on a pole
     is like
a whale in a pail
     is like
a cow on a bough
     is like
a snake in a cake
     is like
a goat in a coat
     is like
a bear in a chair
     is like
an eel at the wheel.

Think of rhymes that give these animals places to be.

A frog on a
            is like
a mouse in a ▢
            is like
a cat on a ▢
            is like
a bug on a ▢
            is like
a snake in a ▢
            is like
a fly on a ▢
            is like
a toad on the ▢.

Can you think of rhymes that make these animals seem like people?

A cat with a ▢
            is like
a bat with a ▢
            is like
a snail with a ▢
            is like
a bee with a ▢
            is like
a sparrow with an ▢
            is like
a raccoon with a ▢
            is like
a pig with a ▢.

13

Look and Tell

Have you ever seen such enormous
boots? Can you imagine anyone wearing
them? Do you think they are real?
What would you do with these boots if
someone gave them to you?

Make up a story about the boots.

Leonard McCombe, Life Magazine © Time, Inc.

Tell
What's
Happening

What's happening here?
What does the bottom
picture tell about the top
one?

Why is everyone watching?
Design a clown's face and
write a funny name for a clown.
Think of something a clown
could do to make people laugh.

Let's Listen

read	run	slide	fall	dive
read	ran	slid	fell	dived or dove
tell	swim	shake	dig	find
told	swam	shook	dug	found

A Story

The Strongest Boy in the World

Look at the pictures. Listen and choose
the best word to complete the story.

Feelings

How do you feel . . .

pleased
annoyed

- when you're waiting for your birthday to come?
- when a riddle is too hard?

confused
sure

- when you lose a dime through a hole in your pocket?
- when you win a prize?

worried
happy

- when someone teases you and you don't like it?
- when there's an exciting crash of thunder and you say, "Pooh, it's nothing but noise!"

patient
impatient

- when you wait for a friend who is late, without complaining?

excited
calm

- when you're certain there are six apples in the refrigerator because you have just counted them?

amused
angry

- when you remember you forgot to feed your dog?
- when you laugh at a TV show?

Can you use the words in the list to tell how you feel about something that happened or might happen to you?

Telling and Asking

A sentence that tells something ends like this .

What does a sentence do that ends like this ?

Do the sentences below tell or ask?

1. Floating an egg is easy.
2. Can you do it?
3. Make a hole in the big end of the egg with a pin.
4. You must make a hole in the little end too.
5. Blow into the first hole.
6. Must you blow hard?
7. If you blow hard enough, the inside of the egg will come out.
8. The egg will float when it's empty.
9. Doesn't it sound easy?

Change the asking sentences to telling sentences. Which of the telling sentences can be changed to questions?

Write two questions that you wish someone would answer. Remember to use question marks.

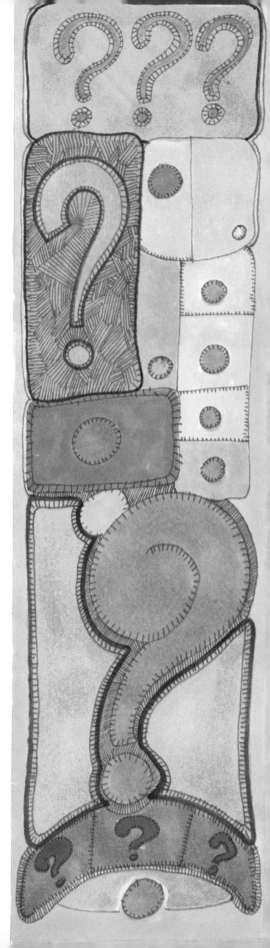

Sentences

Here are seven sentences and one fooler that tell about a game. Find the fooler and make a sentence with the words in it. Then find out how to play the game.

Solemn

- The game Solemn has six or more players.
- players the floor the on sit circle in a
- The players decide who will be the starter.
- The starter tickles the chin of a player next to him.
- That player does the same thing to the next one.
- One by one, all around the circle, chins are tickled.
- Anyone who laughs or smiles or makes a sound is out of the game.
- The last one to stay solemn wins.

20 From *Games of Many Nations* by E. O. Harbin. Copyright 1954 by Pierce and Washabaugh. Reprinted by permission of Abingdon Press.

Why do you think the game is called
Solemn? Play the game and write
sentences about what happens. Or tell
how to play another game.

Word Order

All the sentences on this page can have a different meaning if you change the words around. The first two sentences show how this is done.

The pilot carried the parachute.
The parachute carried the pilot.

Change some of the words around in these sentences and make new sentences.

- The trainer poked the elephant.
- The barber shaved the pig.
- The fox fooled the goose.
- A clown fell on a kettle.
- The baby is afraid of the puppy.
- The wolf nipped the cubs.
- The boy was dressed like a clown.
- The big troll scared the billy goat.

Use each pair of words in a sentence that can be changed around and given a new meaning.

donkey   boys   dog   wolf
man   girls   cat   bear

22

Look and Think

What Did They Say?

Telling Stories

Choose a picture you like.
Tell a story about it.

One day _____

A long time ago _____

Last week _____

One spring morning _____

27

Poems

Shadow Dance

by Ivy O. Eastwick

O, Shadow,
Dear Shadow,
Come, Shadow,
And dance!
On the wall
In the firelight
Let both of
Us prance!
I raise my
Arms, thus!
And you raise
Your arms, so!
And dancing
And leaping
And laughing
We go!
From the wall
To the ceiling,
From ceiling
To wall,
Just you and
I, Shadow,
And none else
At all.

Fun with My Shadow

by Clare Tringress

My shadow walks the way I walk
And runs the way I run,
And if I hop along the road
He hops behind for fun.

I told him just this evening
Before I came to bed,
I thought I'd rather like it
If he went in front instead.

He said,
"Well that's peculiar—
I've often thought it too,——
I've got a big tremendous urge
To show YOU what to do!"

I wonder what he'll show me.
I hope his tricks are new;
I'll learn them really quickly
And show them all to you!

Words for What We Do and Did

take	swing	wear	run	come
took	swung	wore	ran	came

go	see	get	tell	do
went	saw	got	told	did

30

A Story

The Wind and the Loaf

brown

loaf and milk

brown coat silk

goat silky brown please

ground frilly trout sneeze

31

Let's Listen

What Are They Like?

All these poems were made by children.
Each compares things that are different
and tells how they are alike.

Waves

Waves slap on the shore.
And make noises like houses crumbling
many houses falling down.

Carol Moore

Grass

Grass is greener in the spring
It stands up nice and straight
Like tin soldiers at attention.

Jimmy Van Billiard

Dark

Dark fills the sky with his big black cloak.
You never hear him come.
One by one the stars peep through,
Out comes the moon like a big yellow egg.

Beverley Dinsdale

"Waves slap on the shore" and "Dark fills the sky with his big black cloak" from *Miracles: Poems by Children of the English-Speaking World*, collected by Richard Lewis. Copyright, © 1966, by Richard Lewis. Reprinted by permission of Simon & Schuster, Inc. and Penguin Books Ltd.

"Grass is greener . . ." by Jimmy Van Billiard from *Green Is Like a Meadow of Grass*, selected by Nancy Larrick. Copyright © 1968 by Nancy Larrick. Reprinted by permission of Garrard Publishing Company, Champaign, Illinois.

Singing

The children are singing,
their mouths open like sleepy fish.
Our teacher conducting the class
waves her arms
like a rhyme in water.
The girls sing high:
our ears ring for the sweetness.
Listeners stand in dazzling amazement.

Peter Shelton

The White Monster

One morning when I got up
there was a fog.
It looked like a monster
eating up buildings and houses
and cars and trees and roads.
When I walked down the street
the white monster ate me up.

Teresa Trubilla

Make a poem that compares two things
that are different.

Why Rabbit
Has a Short Tail

Make up a how or why story. Choose
a picture from this page or make up your
own story.

How Snake
Lost His Legs

Why It Is Dark at Night

Why a Fly Buzzes

Why Mouse
Is So Small

Why Cat and Dog Hate Each Other

How Fish
Learned to Swim

Why Trees Have
Green Leaves

Riddle Me, Riddle Me, What Is That?

These pages are full of riddles.
Each describes just enough for you to
guess the answer. How many of the
riddles can you solve?

1. Riddle me, riddle me,
      what is that,
   Over the head and
      under the hat?

      (Unknown)

2. Somebody's been in the garden
      Nipping the blossoms fair;
   All the green leaves are blackened;
      Who do you think was there?

      (Unknown)

3. First it was a pretty flower, dressed in pink and white,
   Then it was a tiny ball, almost hid from sight.
   Round and green and large it grew—then it turned to red.
   It will make a splendid pie for your Thanksgiving Spread.

      (Unknown)

From *The Golden Flute*, selected by Alice Hubbard and Adeline Babbitt.
Copyright 1932 by The John Day Company, Inc.

4. A million little diamonds sparkling on the trees,
   And all the children said: "A jewel if you please!"
   But when they stood with hands outstretched
      To catch the jewels gay,
   A million little sunbeams came and took them all away.

(Unknown)

5. There's a flower in the garden,
      It's just like a cup;
   It's yellow, as yellow as butter,
      And they call it_____

(Unknown)

6. First they danced upon the trees,
      Then they floated on the breeze,
   Then they gaily blew around ——
      Now they're sleeping on the ground.

(Unknown)

Make some riddles of your own.

1. hair   2. Jack Frost   3. apple   4. dew   5. buttercup   6. leaves

From *The Golden Flute*, selected by Alice Hubbard and Adeline Babbitt.
Copyright 1932 by The John Day Company, Inc.

Word Order

The words under each riddle tell the
answer if you put them in the right
order. Can you figure out the answers?

1. Why did the teacher wear dark glasses?
       too class bright the was

2. What time is it when an elephant sits
    on a little red wagon?
            wagon is it for a new time

3. What is a baby after it is two years old?
          is years it three old

4. What are little gray cats called in California?
   are they kittens called

5. What do lions have that no other
   animals have?
   lions they little have

6. Why is a library always the highest
   building in town?
   it stories the most has

7. What did the big firecracker say to
   the little firecracker?
   pop pop your my than bigger is

8. What did the donkey say when it was
   caught by the tail?
   me that end the is of

Let's Listen

A Story

Eighteen Rabbits

Writing a Story

Pretend you are in a strange house.
No one has lived in it for a hundred
years. You go into a room, and this
chest seems to be waiting for you. You
open a drawer. What do you find?
What happens next?

Write or tell a story about it.

Opposites

Bob and Bill were twins, but they
were opposites in everything. If you
think of words for the blanks in the
sentences, you will see how opposite
in everything Bob and Bill were.

- Bob was fat, and Bill was ▮▮.

- If Bill went out, Bob came ▮▮.

- When Bob was happy, Bill was ▮▮.

- When Bill was good, Bob was ▮▮.

- If Bob was miserable, Bill was ▮▮.

- When Bill would work, Bob would ▮▮.

- If Bob would go, Bill would ▮▮.

- When Bill was fast, Bob was ▮▮.

- If Bob said yes, Bill said ▮▮.

- When one was up, the other was ▮▮.

- They made their mother smile, but they also made her ▮▮.

What do you think Bob would say if Bill said the words <u>tall</u>, <u>top</u>, <u>little</u>, <u>empty</u>, or <u>hard</u>? What do you think Bill would say if Bob said the words <u>clean</u>, <u>push</u>, <u>big</u>, <u>start</u>, or <u>stupid</u>?

Giving Directions

This crazy little animal was made with a cork, five pins, and a pen. Tell how you would make one like it. Tell what you would do first, next, and last.

Pretend you are telling a blind person how to do one of the things in this list.

- blow bubble gum
- turn a somersault
- mix chocolate milk
- play Hide the Button
- frost a cake
- shine shoes
- make a clay troll
- order a meal in a restaurant
- walk to the principal's office
- draw the flag

Before you give directions, think. Then tell what to do first, next, and last.

Let's Listen

Which Word?

Matt liked his brother Dan and had a habit of repeating everything his brother said. That annoyed Dan.

"Don't be a copycat," Dan said. "If you have to say whatever I say, do it in a different way."

"Ok," said Matt. "I will."

Here are some words that Dan and Matt used to say the same things. One from each list will go in each sentence. Which words are they?

Dan's Words

hustle
wet
begin
frighten
stupid
yelling
good
stop
still
ache

- The show is about to .
- Let's ▢ or we'll be late.
- We must wear boots because it's ▢ outside.
- I wish the girls would stop ▢.
- Silly spooks don't ▢ me.
- It's ▢ to make so much noise.
- Everyone should be ▢ as a mouse.
- The racket makes my head ▢.
- This candy bar tastes ▢.
- I wish this show would never ▢.

Matt's Words

sloppy
start
hurry
screaming
scare
dumb
hurt
delicious
end
quiet

Look and Think

Let's Listen

Let's Think About Words

Which sentences tell where?
Which sentences tell when?

Pete went to play
in the park.

In a few minutes
he met a friend.

The boys did tricks
on the jungle gym.

They were on time
for storytelling.

One of them had fun
at the fountain.

At twelve o'clock
the boys said good-by.

54

Which part of the sentence tells where?

Pete tried to jump
over a puddle.

He flopped
into the water.

Mud splashed
over Pete's clothes.

Some mud was
under his nose.

Pete crawled
out of the puddle.

He washed his face
under a faucet.

55

A Poem

The Goblin
by Rose Fyleman

All {
A goblin lives in <u>our</u> house, in <u>our</u> house, in <u>our</u> house,
A goblin lives in <u>our</u> house all the year round.

He bumps

And he jumps

And he thumps

And he stumps.

He knocks

And he rocks

And he rattles at the locks.

All {
A goblin lives in <u>our</u> house, in <u>our</u> house, in <u>our</u> house,
A goblin lives in <u>our</u> house all the year round.

Have you heard mysterious noises in
your house? Tell about them.

Play the Sentence Game

Begin with a word that tells who.

• Goblins

Add a word that tells what the goblins did.

• Goblins danced.

Add a word that tells how.

• Goblins danced merrily.

Add words that help tell where.

• Goblins danced merrily on the roof.

Add words that help tell when.

• Goblins danced merrily on the roof last night.

Put the words that help tell when first.

Play the game to make up other sentences about goblins. Then play it to make sentences about a giraffe, a merry-go-round, bluebirds, and rain.

Words That Name Sounds

Snap, pop, rattle, roar! There is something alike about all those words. What does each one tell about?

The words at the right tell about sounds made by people, animals, and things. Can you sort them into three lists?

Add to one of the lists the words for the sounds made by dogs, pigs, chickens, turkeys, lions, and pigeons. What are some of the sounds you hear early in the morning, or on a windy day, or on a stormy night?

giggle

mew

tick

chug

cheep

bang

boo

quack

58

Here is a project. Make an ABC book of words for sounds—one word or more for every letter in the alphabet. You will have to listen and look hard for such words. For <u>A</u> you may use the word that means "sneeze." For <u>Z</u> use the word that means "a snore."

To inspire you, below is a very old, funny word for the sound made by frogs.

Poems

Bird Talk
by Aileen Fisher

"Think . . ." said the robin,
"Think . . ." said the jay,
sitting in the garden,
talking one day.

"Think about people—
the way they grow:
they don't have feathers
at all, you know.

"They don't eat beetles,
they don't grow wings,
they don't like sitting
on wires and things.

"Think!" said the robin.
"Think!" said the jay.
"Aren't people funny
to be that way?"

60

"Bird Talk" from *Up the Windy Hill* by Aileen Fisher. Published by Scott, Foresman and Company.

The Turtle

by John Travers Moore

The turtle thinks
   of many things:
He thinks of bugs
   with glassy wings,

He thinks of minnows
   in a school,
He thinks of lilies
   on the pool.

But he thinks long
   and he thinks well
Before he comes
   out of his shell!

"The Turtle" by John T. Moore from *Story Parade* copyright 1954 by Story Parade, Inc. Reprinted by permission of Western Publishing Company, Inc.

A Poem

Sebastian and the Dragon

Why did Sebastian go on a journey?
What did all the things on this page
have to do with his journey?
Why did Sebastian and the dragon
like each other?
How did Sebastian become a hero in
his home town?
What was Sebastian's reward?

Letter Writing

Charlie Gets a Letter from the Moon

by James Flora

"I got a letter from the moon today," my friend Charlie said. "Do you want to know what it says?"

"Sure," I said. "I never heard from the moon in my whole life."

"It says, 'Dear Charlie: I saw you the other night when you stayed up until ten-thirty playing hide-and-seek. That is too late, and your mother was worried. I hope you won't do that again.

'And why do you keep telling people that I am made of green cheese when you know very well that I'm made of rocks? Please tell the truth about me.

'Thanks for sending me all the doughnuts and gumdrops last week. They were very good. I don't get much good food up here except when some kind friend remembers to send me some.

'Can you come up here for a visit next week? It would be nice to have you. Bring your pajamas, and you can bring your friend George if you like.

Sincerely,

your friend The Moon

'P.S. Please bring some new flashlight batteries when you come. I think mine are wearing out. I don't seem to shine as brightly as I did last year.'"

"That's goofy," I said. "How can you go to the moon? How can the moon eat gumdrops? And you know very well he doesn't need batteries to shine. Where did you get that crazy letter, Charlie?"

"I made it up," said Charlie. "I always wanted a letter from the moon, but I never got one until today. I think I'll go. Do you want to go along?"

We went and had a wonderful time. Just make believe, of course.

Charlie's letter was in a story.
This is how a letter might look on
Moon writing paper.

Saturday

Dear Jane,

It was chilly last night.
It was 200 degrees below
zero. Wear warm clothes if
you visit me at night.

With love,
The Moon

P.S. It is 200 degrees above
zero today.

A Poem

Little Talk

by Aileen Fisher

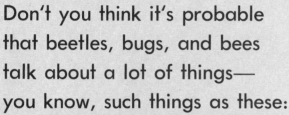

Don't you think it's probable
that beetles, bugs, and bees
talk about a lot of things—
you know, such things as these:

The kind of weather where they live
in jungles tall with grass
and earthquakes in their villages
whenever people pass!

Of course we'll never know if bugs
talk very much at all,
because our ears are far too big
for talk that is so small.

Can you imagine yourself as little as
a bug and make up some bug talk? Pretend
you are a bee or a greedy mosquito or a
cricket with a transistor radio. Write
some sentences that you would say.

"Little Talk" by Aileen Fisher from *That's Why*, published by Thomas Nelson & Sons, N.Y., 1946.
Reprinted by permission of the author.

Making Sentences

A sentence is more than a group of any old words. When the words are put together, they must tell something. On page 69 match the words on the left with the words on the right. You can make ten sentences that tell a story.

Snow White
and the
Seven Dwarfs

Bob and Betty	were pink
its eyes	had a white mouse
its name	lived in a cage
Snow White	was Snow White
one day Snow White	looked everywhere for Snow White
the children	was lost
after a while they	seven baby mice
with Snow White were	found her in the sewing basket
Betty	said, Eek, eek, eek, eek, eek, eek, eek
the babies	said, Let's call them The Seven Dwarfs

Do you know another story called
"Snow White and the Seven Dwarfs"? How
is that story different from this one?

Be a Word Collector

Harvey
collects
rocks.

May
collects
pennies.

Henrietta
collects dolls
from different
countries.

Do you have a collection?
Tell about it.

David keeps his collection in a little
notebook. One page begins like this.

Happy Words	Sad Words
fortunate	unfortunate
laughter	moan
melody	starving
orange	whimper
cuddly	
tickle	

Another page begins like this.

Beautiful Words	Interesting Words
star	astonish
shadowy	shaggy
misty	crackle
melody	hubbub
	prickly
	lukewarm

What did David collect?
How can David use his
collection?

A Poem

Houses

by Mary Britton Miller

The homes of our
Earliest ancestors
Were lower than low,
They had no windows,
They had no doors.
If you wished to go in
You went on all fours—
The dirt or the dust
Or the snow was the floor.
It was hundreds and hundreds
Of years before
Men lived in houses
With windows and doors
Or lay down in beds
Or sat up in chairs
Or sat down at table
Or walked upstairs:

Then, as time goes,
It was no time at all
Before houses were built
So exceedingly tall,
They had hundreds of windows
And only one door
And you had to go up
In an elevator.
And now they have grown
So gigantically high
They nudge the new moon
And scrape the blue sky;
And today we live
Like bees in a hive
In the tallest cities
That Mister Man
Has built on this earth
Since the world began.

Who is Mister Man?
What kind of buildings "scrape the
blue sky"?
What kind of house do you live in?
Write some sentences about your
house or a house you'd like to live in.

73

If I Were . . .

If I were a
fairy godmother,
I would   .

If I were
a wizard, I
would   .

What would you like to pretend being?
What would you do then?

Let's Listen

Read what Anne told her mother about her fishing trip. What words did she use?

tell	know
told	knew
do	sit
did	sat
throw	catch
threw	caught
bring	take
brought	took
buy	
bought	

- I ▭ daddy I ▭ all about fishing, and I proved it.
- I ▭ everything he told me to do.
- I ▭ quietly.
- I ▭ my hook into the water myself.
- I ▭ all my fish with the secret bait I ▭.
- I ▭ the fish off the hook by myself.
- Daddy ▭ his fish with his hands.
- On the way home he ▭ me a double chocolate malted.

A Poem

The Animal Store

by Rachel Field

If I had a hundred dollars to spend,
    Or maybe a little more,
I'd hurry as fast as my legs would go
    Straight to the animal store.

I wouldn't say, "How much for this or that?"—
    "What kind of a dog is he?"
I'd buy as many as rolled an eye,
    Or wagged a tail at me!

I'd take the hound with the drooping ears
    That sits by himself alone;
Cockers and Cairns and wobbly pups
    For to be my very own.

I might buy a parrot all red and green,
    And the monkey I saw before,
If I had a hundred dollars to spend,
    Or maybe a little more.

Suppose you could buy any pet you wanted at the animal store. Finish these sentences to tell what you would buy.

- I would like to buy ▆▆ because ▆▆.
- I would like to buy ▆▆ if ▆▆.
- I would like to buy ▆▆ but ▆▆.

Using Different Words

One day Hal and his brother Joe found a snake. Here is what Hal told their sister Sarah.

"Mom is <u>furious</u> because we <u>caught</u> a snake under the front steps. The snake <u>frightens</u> her, but we <u>love</u> it. I think we'll <u>call</u> him Henry. We'll <u>make</u> him a cage. But <u>maybe</u> he'll wiggle out. Oh dear, now mother is so upset she's <u>crying</u>. We'll have to <u>free</u> our beautiful snake."

When Joe told their father about the snake he used different words. Which words might Joe have used in place of the underlined words?

scares	release	angry
name	weeping	captured
build	perhaps	adore

Let's
Listen

Asking or Telling

Do these sentences ask or tell?
What mark goes at the end?

Jim said, "Look at these sticks ☐
Do you know what they are ☐ "

Linda said, "They are drumsticks ☐
Do you have a little drum, Jim ☐ "

Jim said, "They are not drumsticks ☐
Can't you guess, Linda ☐ "
Linda said, "They must be lollipop sticks ☐
Did you eat the lollipops off them ☐ "
Jim laughed, "They are chopsticks ☐
I eat with them ☐ "
Linda said, "How do you do that ☐
Do you use both hands ☐ "
Jim said, "Like this ☐
See ☐ "

A Poem

I Don't Understand

by Vivian Gouled

These are some things
I don't understand . . .

Why rocks are hard,
    What makes the sand,
Why stems are green,
    Why rabbits hop,
Why ocean tides
    won't ever stop;
How we remember
    or forget,
Why dew and rain
    and snow are wet,
What makes a puppy
    like to play . . .
I hope to learn these things
    some day!

You and your class write a poem about
some things you don't understand. Your
poem need not rhyme.

A Puppet Show

Once there were two puppets. The big puppet was named Me-me. The little one was named Me-too.

Me-me said, "I want to go downtown."

"I want to go downtown too," said Me-too.

"First I'm going to buy a racing car," said Me-me.

"I'm going to buy a racing car too," said Me-too.

"Then I'll have two ice-cream cones for lunch," said Me-me.

"I'll have two ice-cream cones too," said Me-too.

"Last, I will go to the dentist and get my tooth pulled," said Me-me.

"I'll get my tooth—Oh no, not me!" said Me-too. "That is too much. Good-by, good-by."

Make up your own puppet shows about Me-me and Me-too.

Let's Listen

Finishing Sentences

My name is Bossy because I tell when to get up and when to go to bed.

1. My name is Curious because  .

2. My name is Question because .

3. My name is Noisy
   because ▢.

4. My name is Pancake
   because ▢.

5. My name is Speedy
   because ▢.

6. My name is Clumsy
   because ▢.

Where Is It?

in   underneath   between   beneath

beside   inside   under   over

above   next to   on   behind

           in back of   in front of

Study the picture on page 86. What is the missing word or phrase in each sentence below? The words at the top of page 86 will help you.

The children are standing ☐ the window.

The boy is standing ☐ the girls.

The trash can is ☐ the children.

The broken airplane is ☐ the trash can.

The teddy bear is ☐ the tricycle.

The rocking chair is ☐ the doll.

The doll is holding an umbrella ☐ her head.

The clown doll is standing ☐ the girl doll.

The man is ☐ the store.

The sign Toy Store is ☐ the store window.

The Golden Goose

Once upon a time there were three brothers. The youngest one was called Simplekin, and everybody made fun of him.

One day the oldest brother was going to the forest to cut wood. His mother gave him a large cake for his lunch. In the forest he met an old man who said, "I'm very hungry. Can you spare a morsel?"

"Certainly not!" the oldest brother replied. "I've just enough for myself." He began to chop down a tree, but his ax slipped. He cut his arm and had to go home without any wood.

The next day the second brother went to the forest. He, too, was given a large cake. He, too, met the old man and refused him anything to eat. When he began to chop a tree, he slashed his leg and could hardly walk home.

The next morning Simplekin went to cut wood, but he was given a tiny burnt cake. He met the old man who said he was hungry. "I have just this burnt cake," said Simplekin, "but we will share it."

The old man said, "You are very kind. I want to reward you. Chop down that tree and you will find a treasure."

Simplekin chopped. And out of the tree stepped a shining golden goose.

Simplekin started for home with the goose under his arm. As he was passing an inn, three sisters saw him. Each of them wanted a feather from the golden goose. The oldest sister touched the bird and could not pull her hand away. Her sisters touched her and stuck fast.

Simplekin kept on walking. A parson tried to free the girls, but stuck fast to them. His clerk reached out a helping hand and he was stuck too. Two farmers tried to help and were joined to the crowd trailing the goose.

They all came to a city where there lived a princess who never had laughed. The king had promised that whoever made her laugh could marry her. When she saw the trail of people behind Simplekin, she laughed so hard she couldn't stop. She and Simplekin were married, and they lived merrily ever after.

Think of other people who might have got stuck to the goose. Act out the story.

SWIMMING POOL

Children's Zoo

MAY

1	2	3	4	5	6	7
8	9	10	11	12	13	14
15	16	17	18	19	20	21
22	23	24	25	26	27	28
29	30	31				

Some Words Help
Tell Where or When

always   to the swimming pool
sometimes   on him
on Saturdays   from the window
later   into the water
last week   on the bottom
in a few minutes   by the pool
just then   to the zoo
three o'clock   on the street

Which of the words above tell where and which tell when? Tell which ones will go into the following sentences.

▭ my friend and I go ▭.
My mother ▭ waves to me ▭.
▭ I left a quarter ▭.
▭ a boy kicked it ▭.
My friend floated by ▭ and the quarter landed ▭.

Write three sentences that tell where and when.

Writing Stories

A good story usually tells all you want to know. Which of these stories don't tell enough?

The Tree

Every day when I go to school I pass a big old tree that leans. I run up the trunk as far as I can and then I run down. One day something happened. I crashed down. It felt as if the tree hit me. I got a bump on my head and a scrape on my cheek. But I still run up the tree every day.

The Lost Cat and Kitten

One morning there were funny mewing sounds in our kitchen. Our cat had three kittens. They were so cute, but my mother said we must not touch them until they were bigger.

One day the cat disappeared with one of the kittens. We looked and looked and looked all over the house. No cat and no kitten. At last we found them.

Sandy's Umbrella

One day Sandy found an umbrella with a hole in it. She liked to look through the hole in the umbrella when she was out walking, but when it rained she got wet.

Sandy's mother gave her some plastic. Together they sewed it over the hole. Now Sandy has an umbrella with a window in it.

The Giant

Once upon a time there was a giant rabbit one hundred feet high. He was so tall he couldn't reach down and nibble grass. He had to eat the tops of trees and that gave him a stomach ache.

One day he was walking along and holding his stomach. He met a boy and girl. They asked him what was the matter, and he told them.

"We'll help you," the boy and girl said. And so they did.

You tell a story.

Answer the Questions

What will he do?

What did he do?

What will she do?

What did she do?

What will he do?

What did he do?

What will Rip do?

What did Rip do?

What will the king do?

What did the king do?

What will she do?

What did she do?

Photograph by Arnold Zann

Look and Think

Is somebody in trouble?

Tell what is happening now.

What do you think happened before?

What will happen next?

A Modern Ballad

The Ups and Downs of the Elevator Car

by Caroline D. Emerson

The elevator car in the elevator shaft,
Complained of the buzzer, complained of the draft.
It said it felt carsick as it rose and fell,
It said it had a headache from the ringing of the bell.

"There is spring in the air," sighed the elevator car.
Said the elevator man, "You are well-off where you are."
The car paid no attention but it frowned an ugly frown

```
                          when
                up        it
           going              should
      started                       be
    it                                  going
And                                        down.
```

<u>Down</u> flashed the signal, but <u>up</u> went the car.
The elevator man cried, "You are going much too far!"
Said the elevator car, "I'm doing no such thing.
I'm through with buzzers buzzing. I'm looking for the spring!"

Then the elevator man began to shout and call
And all the people came running through the hall.
The elevator man began to call and shout.
"The car won't stop! Let me out! Let me out!"

On went the car past the penthouse door.
On went the car up one flight more.
On went the elevator till it came to the top.
On went the elevator, and it would not stop!

Right through the roof went the man and the car.
And nobody knows where the two of them are!
(Nobody knows but everyone cares,
Wearily, drearily climbing the stairs!)

Now on a summer evening when you see a shooting star
Fly through the air, perhaps it is—that elevator car!

How Do You Know It's Spring?

Michael Mauney, *Life* Magazine © Time Inc.

Spring makes me feel like . . .
In spring I feel as gay as . . .
In spring I feel as peppy as . . .

Michael Mauney, *Life* Magazine © Time Inc.

Punctuation

Look at the marks before and after the next word—"Hello!" Those small slant lines are quotation marks.

This joke shows what quotation marks tell a reader.

John brought four friends home with him. They had been to the zoo.

"These boys caused an awful commotion at the zoo, father," he said.

"Boys, I want each of you to tell me your names and what you did to cause the commotion," said John's father.

"My name is George, and I threw peanuts into the elephant pen," said the first boy.

"My name is Pete, and I threw peanuts into the elephant pen," said the second boy.

"My name is Dick, and I threw peanuts into the elephant pen," said the third boy.

"My name is Peanuts," said the fourth boy.

Act out the joke as if it were a play.

Quotation marks have been left out
of these jokes. Where should they be?

I know how you tell if an elephant
has been in the refrigerator, said Daffy.
Tell me, said Dilly.
Look for his footprints in the
butter, said Daffy.

I know how to tell when there is an
elephant in your sandwich, said Dilly.
Tell me, said Daffy.
When the sandwich is too heavy to
lift, said Dilly.

Denny's father gave him two goldfish
for his birthday.
Take good care of them, said Denny's
father.
The next day Denny's father said,
Did you give your fish fresh water today?
They haven't finished the water they
got yesterday, said Denny.

A Weary Word

Which words can be used instead of
<u>nice</u> in this story?

pretty
gentle
sunny

One day Joe went to the zoo with
forty boys and girls. It was a nice day.
A nice breeze was blowing. The flower
beds looked very nice.

funny

interesting

handsome

entertaining

clean

restful

attractive

pleasant

exciting

The boys and girls walked for miles and saw dozens of animals. Joe thought all the animals were nice. The monkeys were nice. The tigers were nice. It was nice to watch the seals dive and swim.

Joe got tired and lagged behind the group. He wished he could have a nice sleep. He came to a nice little building and looked in. He saw a room full of empty cages. The floor of one cage was covered with nice straw, and the door was open.

Joe climbed into the cage. He was having a nice dream when he heard someone say, "Be careful. This animal is dangerous."

Joe was scared. He opened his eyes, and forty children laughed at him. They said Joe had given their trip a nice ending, but Joe wasn't sure he agreed.

A Poem

"I Can't" Said the Ant

by Polly Cameron

I was taking a walk
When I heard a loud clatter!
I rushed into the kitchen
To see what was the matter.

There on the floor
With the tea pouring out
Was a cracked teapot
With a broken spout.

"Good heavens! What happened,
My poor Miss Teapot?"
She rolled over and murmured,
"The tea was too hot."

"What's all the clatter?" asked the platter.
"Teapot fell," said the dinner bell.
"Teapot broke," said the artichoke.
"She went kerplop!" said the mop.
"Is she dead?" asked the bread.
"Just a break," said the steak.
"Broke her spout," said the trout.

106

"A fine fettle," said the kettle.
"Alas," said the glass.
"What a life," said the knife.
"Push her up," said the cup.
"I can't," said the ant.
"You can," said the pan.
"You must," said the crust.
"Please try," said the pie.
"That's the way," said the tray.
"That's good!" said the wood.
"Higher," said the fire.
"It's a breeze," said the cheese.
"You've gone far," said the jar.
"They slid," said the lid.
"How exhausting," said the frosting.
"Relax," said the ax.
"Stop and think," said the sink.

If you could think like an ant, how
would you rescue the teapot?
Imagine a thermometer has fallen to
the floor of your room. Make rhymes
like those in the poem to tell what other
things might say. Start with the door,
if you like.

A Story

Georgie Finds a Grandpa

Did you ever want something very much?
How did you try to get it?

Words Describe

Describe one of the birds well enough
for the class to know which bird you're
talking about.

Do you know your state bird? What is it?

Writing Invitations

What?

Where?

When?

Who?

You are invited to
a wiener roast
at 1223 Drexel Street
Saturday at noon

Judy Johnson

You're invited to a Splash Party!

When?
1:00 P.M.
Saturday
May 4

Where?
32 Oak Lane

Who?
John Carter

Bring your
swimsuit

Maxie
needs a new home.
Come to a
Doghouse Building Party
Saturday, June 5
at 12 noon
behind Ted's house

My dad will help!

Bring your own straw
and come to my

Soda Tasting Party

Come thirsty
on Thursday
at 3:30 P.M.
Suzy's house

201 Elm Street

What kind of party
would you like to have?
Make an invitation
for it.

Let's Listen

Mr. Groundhog Turns Around

Why was Mr. Groundhog shivering?
Do you know what frightened him?
Do you know of any other old beliefs
or superstitions? Tell about them.

Look
and
Write

Three of these
children seem to
be planning to get
something out of
the water. What
is it? How can it
be brought to land?
Write or tell a
story about what
happened.

Photograph by Arnold Zann

Poems

boys {
The pickety fence
The pickety fence
Give it a lick it's
The pickety fence

girls {
Give it a lick it's
A clickety fence
Give it a lick it's
A lickety fence

boys {
Give it a lick
Give it a lick
Give it a lick
With a rickety stick

girls {
Pickety
Pickety
Pickety
Pick

by David McCord

Grandfather Frog

by Louise Seaman Bechtel

girls
: Fat green frog sits by the pond,
Big frog, bull frog, grandfather frog.

boys
: Croak—croak—croak.

girls
: Shuts his eye, opens his eye,
Rolls his eye, winks his eye,
Waiting for
A little fat fly.

boys
: Croak, croak.

girls
: I go walking down by the pond,
I want to see the big green frog,
I want to stare right into his eye,
Rolling, winking, funny old eye.

solo
: But oh! he hears me coming by.

boys
: Croak—croak—

all
: SPLASH!

Stories to Finish

One day Matt was kicking a can along an alley between high wooden fences. He was lonesome.

The can rattled against one of the fences and Matt went over to give it another kick. Then he noticed the fence had a hole in it just the size of a human eye. Over the fence came sounds of music and laughter. Matt put his eye to the hole and smiled.

What do you think he saw?

Liz wanted a pet, but she had a problem. Cats made her father sneeze. Her mother was afraid of dogs. Her sister was afraid of mice. Her brother objected to birds, and her grandfather objected to fish. Liz herself liked anything that moved.

In the summer Liz went to camp. When she came home she brought a tiny pet with her.

What was the pet?

Katie had a toothache, but she wouldn't go to the dentist. Her mother took her anyway, but Katie wouldn't open her mouth.

The dentist looked at Katie kindly. Then he opened a drawer and showed her something. "Will this help?" he asked.

What do you think he gave Katie?

Tom was taking a slow walk past the house of his old friend Mr. Dodge. He was hoping Mr. Dodge would invite him in for some root beer, and that's what happened.

"I need your advice, Tom," said Mr. Dodge. "I'm going to move away, and I don't know what to do with my old car. It's fifty years old and will never run again, but I like it. I'd like to give it to someone who'd like it as much as I do. Have you any ideas?"

Tom sipped his root beer and thought. Suddenly he had the greatest idea of his entire life.

What do you think it was?

Making Sentences

Can you see pictures in the lines on this page? Write sentences about what you see in them. Here is an example: Charlie was cheerful, but Mike was mad. Can you find Charlie and Mike? Use your imagination and see how many sentences you can write.

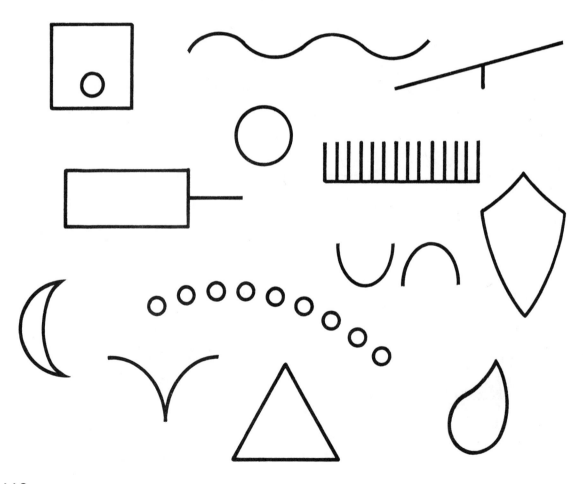

Let's Listen

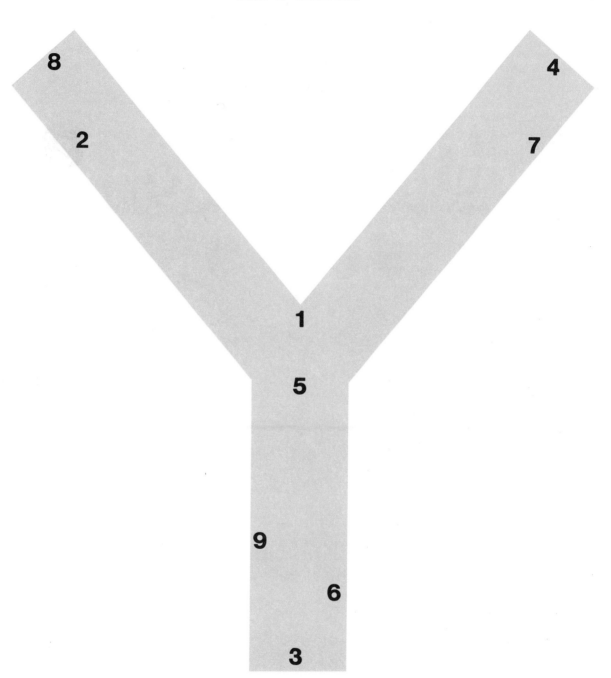

Can you find your way?
Can you remember every landmark?

Punctuation

Gerald and Deborah were talking about stories they liked.

Gerald said, "I like the story about the golden goose best. It's so funny when everyone gets stuck to the goose."

"I liked that story where everything could talk. Wouldn't it be strange if the stones and trees and animals could talk?" Deborah asked.

"What fun!" said Gerald. "I wonder what that tree outside our window would tell us."